TEA LEAVES

TEA LEAVES

History and Delights of Tea Drinking

Enjoy!
Barbara Larsen
Gretchen Maring

Poems by Barbara Larsen
Illustrations by Gretchen Maring

First Edition
All rights reserved

Copyright © 1999 Barbara Larsen
Illustrations © copyright 1999 Gretchen Maring

No part of this book may be reproduced in any form or by any means, electronic or mechanical, including photocopying, without permission of the copyright holders.

ISBN 0-9671668-0-2

Library of Congress
Catalog Card Number 99-62490

Published by
Beach Road Press
11751 Beach Road
Sister Bay, WI 54234

For George and John,
our favorite tea drinking companions

Camellia sinensis

茶

Ch'a

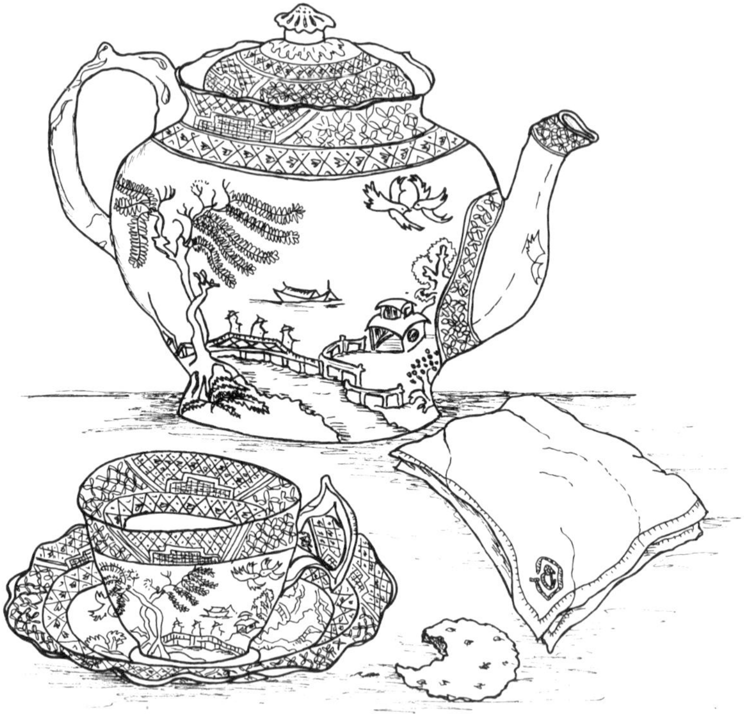

Come in!

Share a cup of tea
let clear warmth
seep into chilled bones

Trade village gossip
everyday stories
the deer who leaped the road
steam rising from the bay

Let this moment embroider itself
into your life with simple stitches

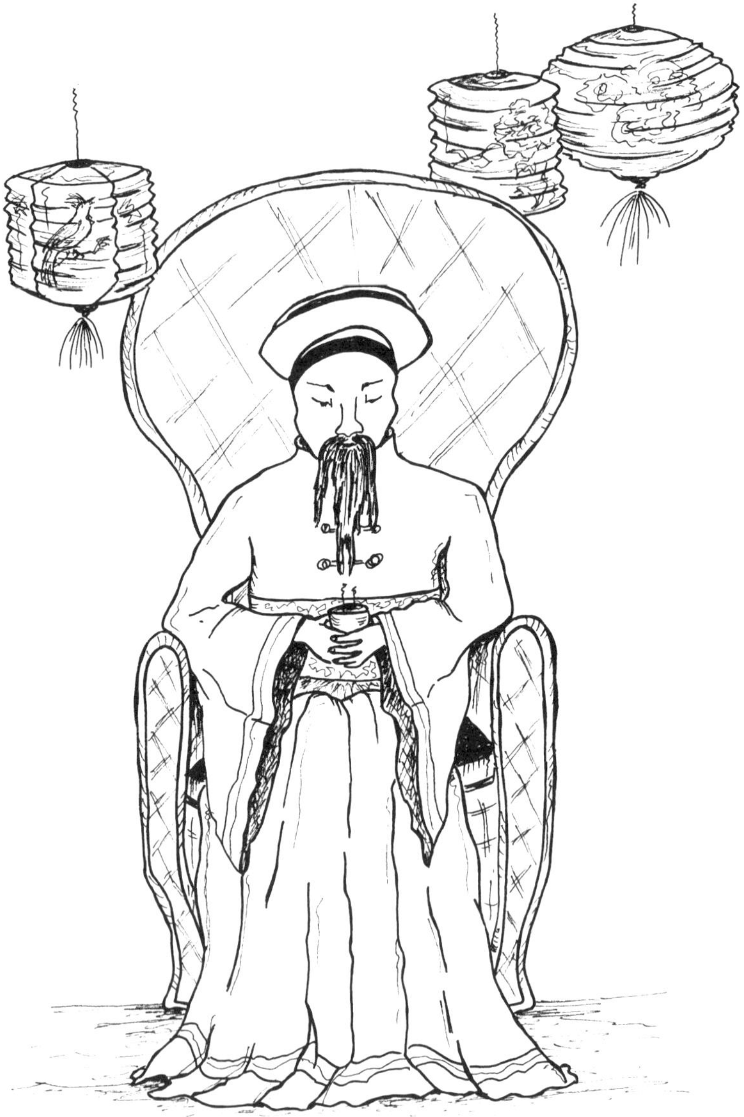

Perhaps...

          a butterfly fluttering up
from heather on a Stone Age moor
set in motion the tiny breeze that,
traveling over continent and ocean,
brushed a leaf from a tea plant
into a pot of boiling water in China.

Picture Emperor Shen Nung
meditating in his garden of tranquility.
Becoming aware of a new aroma,
he summons his servant to bring a cup.

Imagine his tentative sip,
the smile and sigh of pleasure
as the world's first cup of tea
is savored in 2737 B.C.

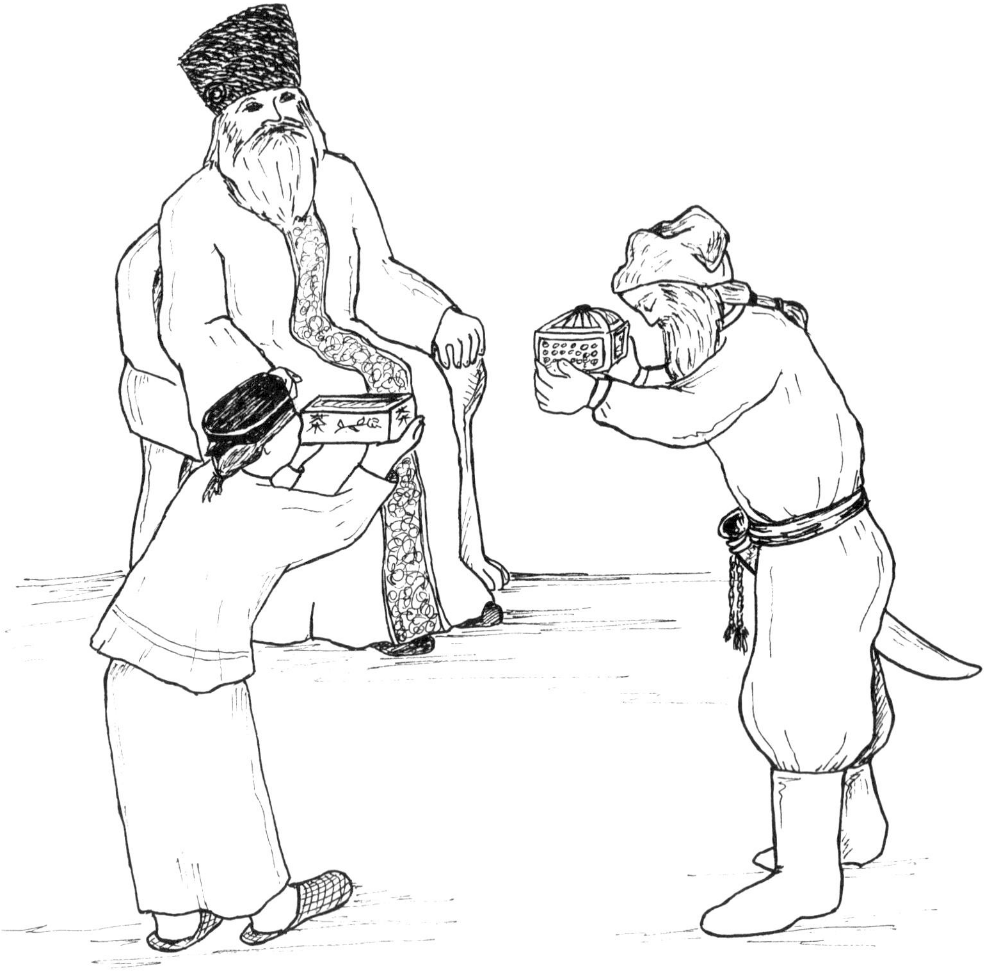

Origins

No one knows for sure:
the jungles of Assam, India?
   the Bohea Mountains of China?
     the Yangtze Valley in Szechwan?

Somewhere tiny roots took hold,
  grew into tender green plants,
    evolved into a drink of comfort and pleasure:
      a welcome immigrant to continents,
        a stake in economic and political affairs.

While scholars debated origins,
  Chinese emperors sipped Tribute Tea,
    Ch'an Buddhists practiced tea rituals,
      ambassadors brought tea to the Russian tsar
        and Americans in feathered headdresses
          dumped tea in Boston harbor.

Su Tung-po's Instructions for Making Tea

Take water from running stream
    from spring in mountains best
    river water will do
    well water poor.

Boil over lively fire
    clear bright charcoal fire.
Do not boil hastily.

At first water sparkles like crab's eyes
    then like eye of fish
        at last it bubbles like pearls innumerable
            leaping, waving about.

NOW is time to make infusion.

    - based upon Su Tung-p'o's writings (1036-1101)

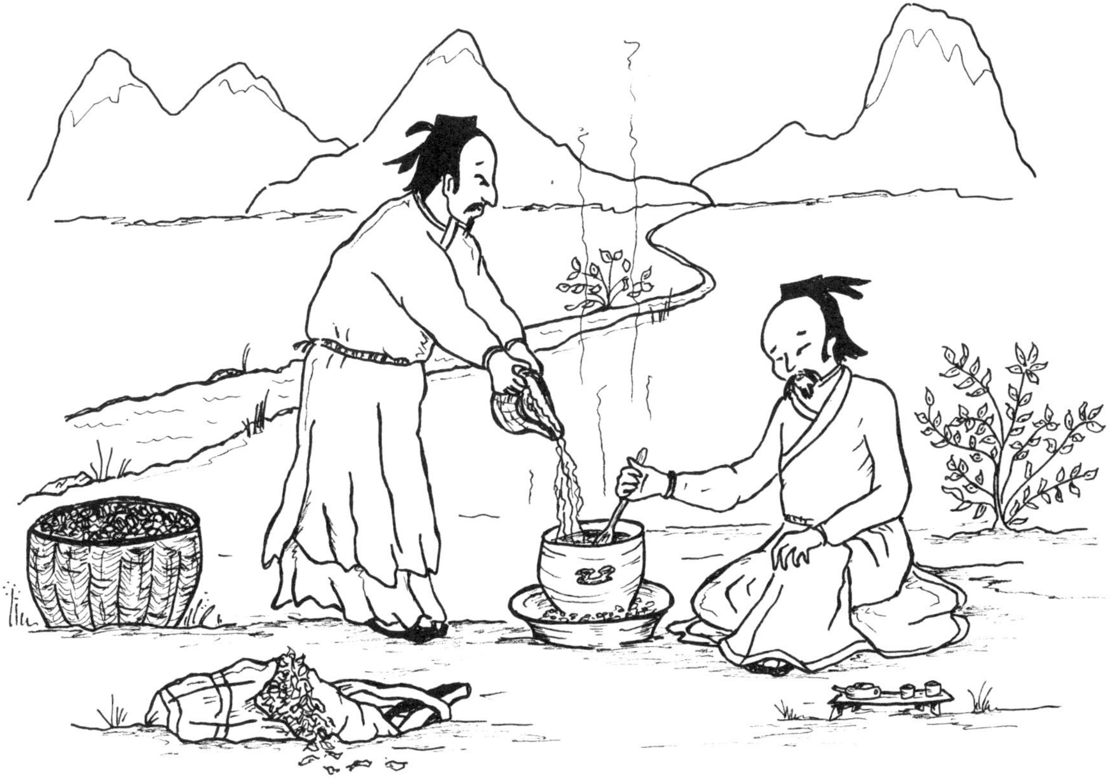

On summer days

                in a pavilion
            overlooking pools where golden fish
      swim among the lotus flowers
a Chinese grandmother
      pours tea for granddaughters
        tells them legends
of teas named Bright Virtue
    Cloud Mist
        and Water Nymph

small grandson begs for Dragon's Well
    on his day
        to visit

Pu-erh Ch'a (Trouser-seat tea)

       While the overseer
nips at their heels,
young girls
pick wild tea
for rich landowners,
long for day's end.
Bowls of rice wait in the village.

       When his back is turned
they hide leaves
in the seats
of their wide trousers
to sell in secret.

       With heads bowed
they exchange
  small
    sidelong
      glances.

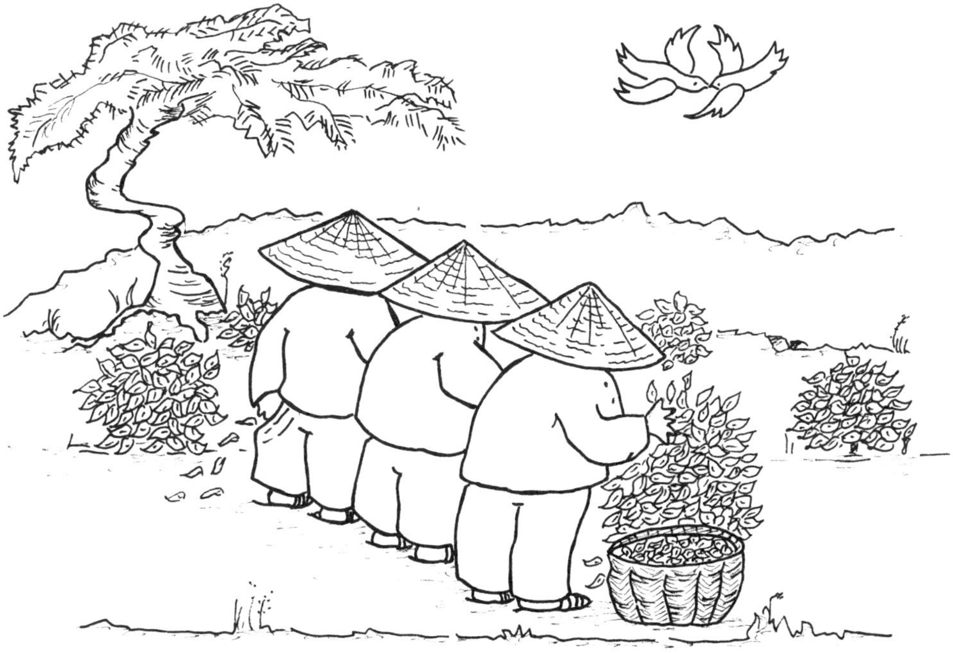

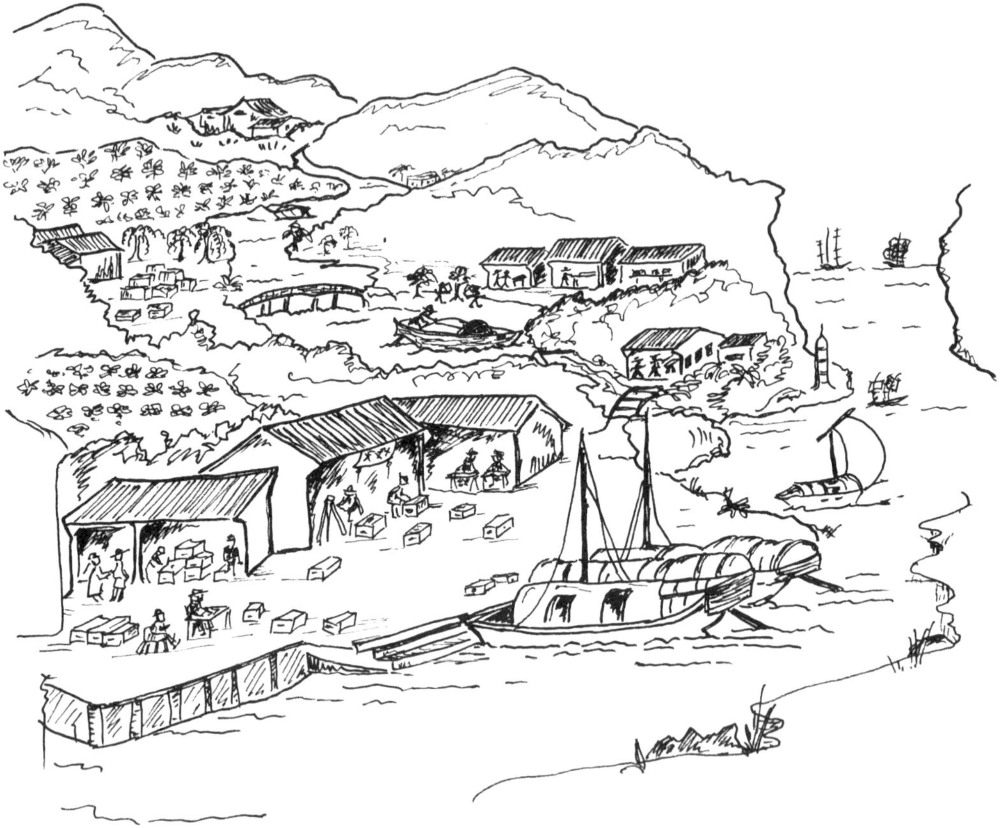

The 1598 Voyage of Hugo Van Linschoten

A Dutch trader sails to the Far East
eager to turn a profit.
Gold doubloons shine in his eyes
as he explores Macao warehouses,
negotiates with Portuguese merchants,
sips cups of a strange and pleasant drink.
While his ship's hold fills with silks and spices
he writes, in English:

The Voyages and Travels
of
Hugo Van Linschoten.

extolling the new substance, Ch'a.
European curiosity starts to brew.

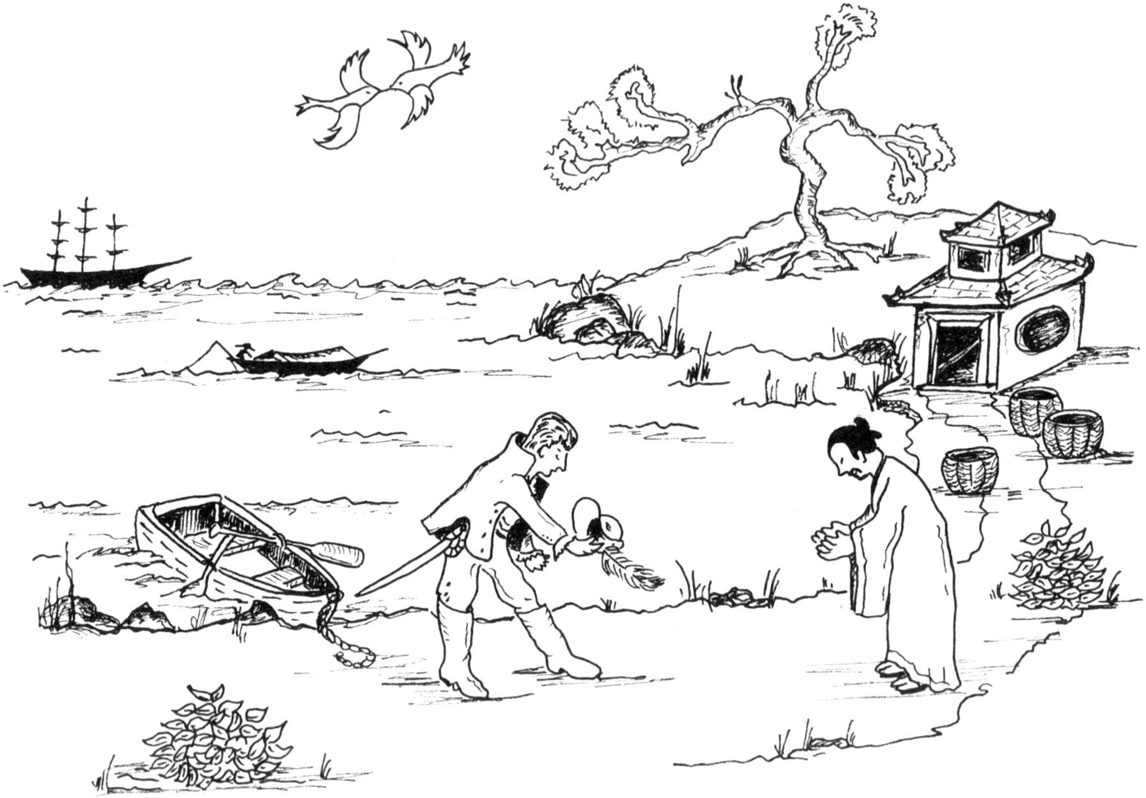

Cha-shitsu

Long before karyukai,
the flower and willow world of the geisha,
before tea was served in houses crowding
narrow-as-an-eel's-bed block in Pontocha,
Sen-no Rikyu, aesthete, built the first tea house
where men of culture could share tea, admire beauty,
painting, calligraphy, flowers,
write haiku and invite, upon occasion,
the captain of a silk-laden Portuguese Great Ship
to approach by dewy path the Cha-shitsu,
sit as honored guest, and experience
the serenity and delicate rituals
of Chado--way of tea.

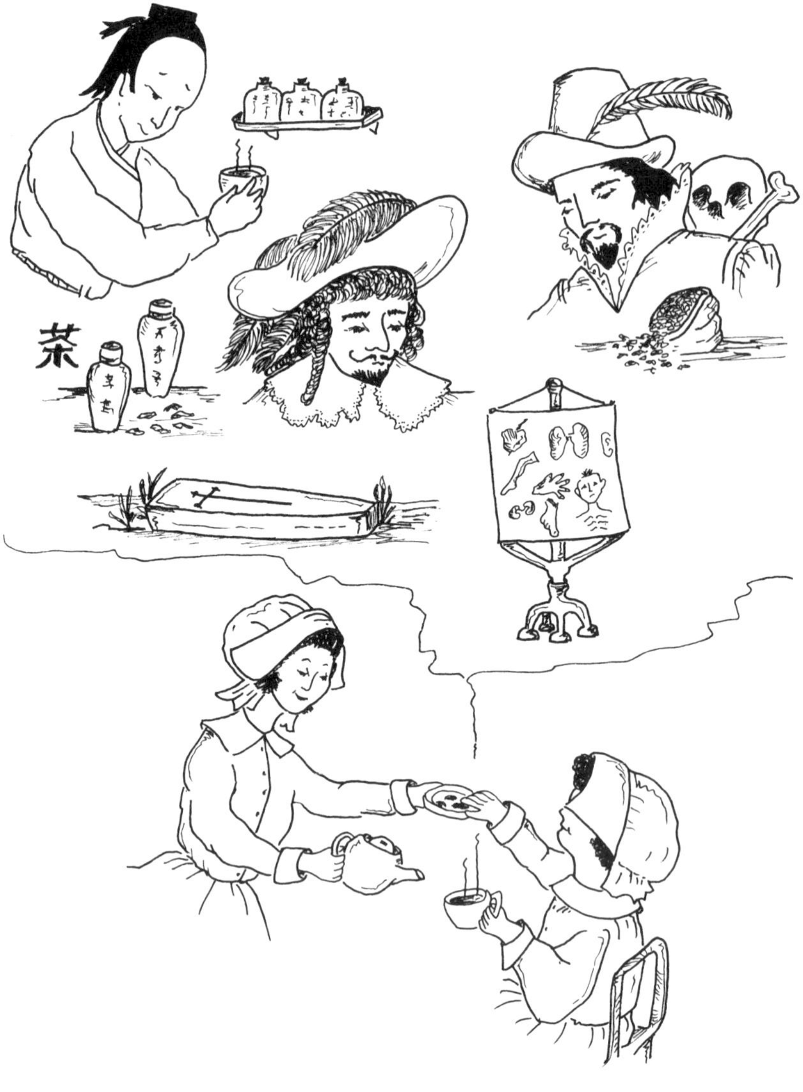
茶

The Great Debate

A medicinal elixir as the Chinese say?
Dr. Simon Paulli, German coffee drinker,
says, "Nein!" and publishes a treatise to that effect.

Dutch physician Nikolas Dirx counters:
"Drinkers of tea will be exempt from all maladies;
will reach an extreme old age."

The debate of the 1600's rages:

    "Tea--panacea for ills of spleen,
        kidneys, and other organs. It cures colds!"

            "Tea causes premature death!"

Not caring a whit, Charles II and his Catherine
serve tea with style to courtiers in the red drawing room.
Soon footmen and housemaids are retrieving the dregs
and sipping away in the kitchen.

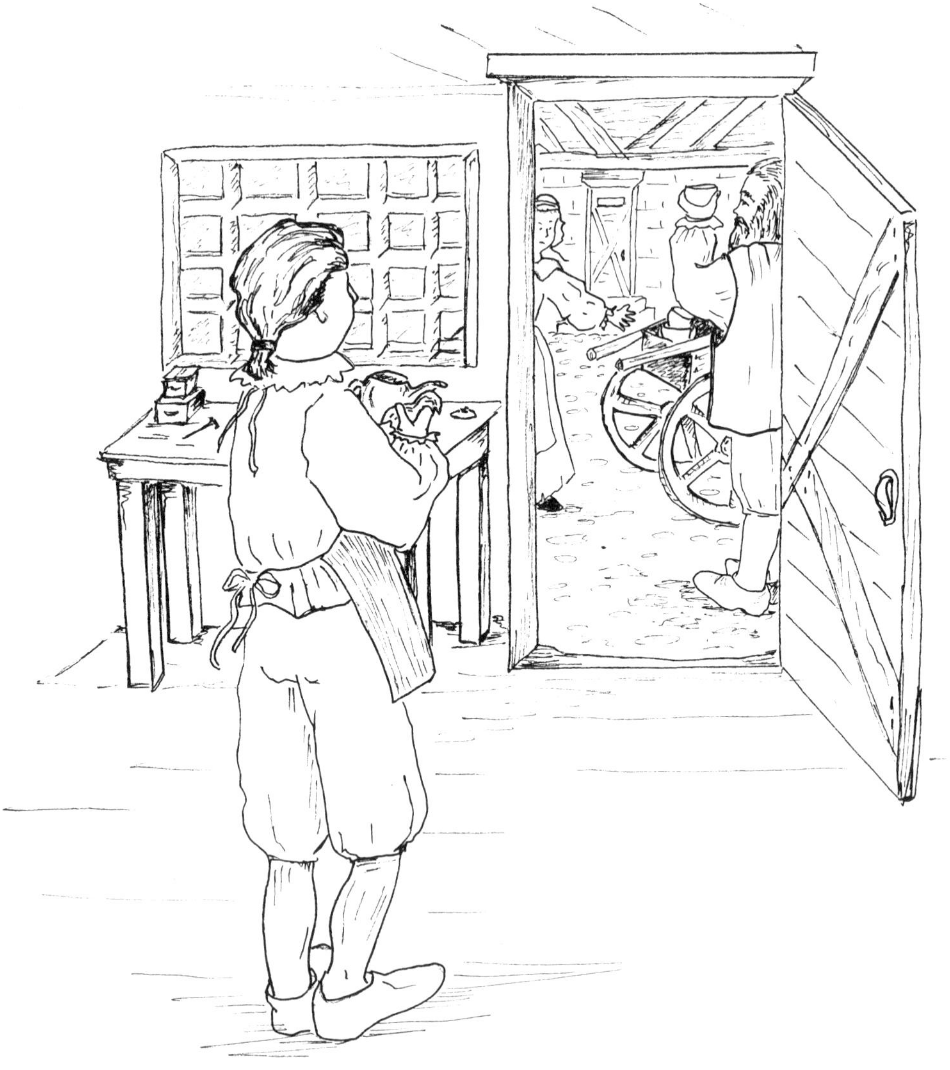

Dutchess of York

While English smiths craft silver teapots,
trying to make the perfect server,
the Dutchess of York brings tea to Scotland.
Just back from Amsterdam,
she tells of tea shops with samples to taste,
vendors selling tea with milk from wheelbarrows,
and burghers irritable without their morning t'ay!
Conservative Scots take their time to be convinced.

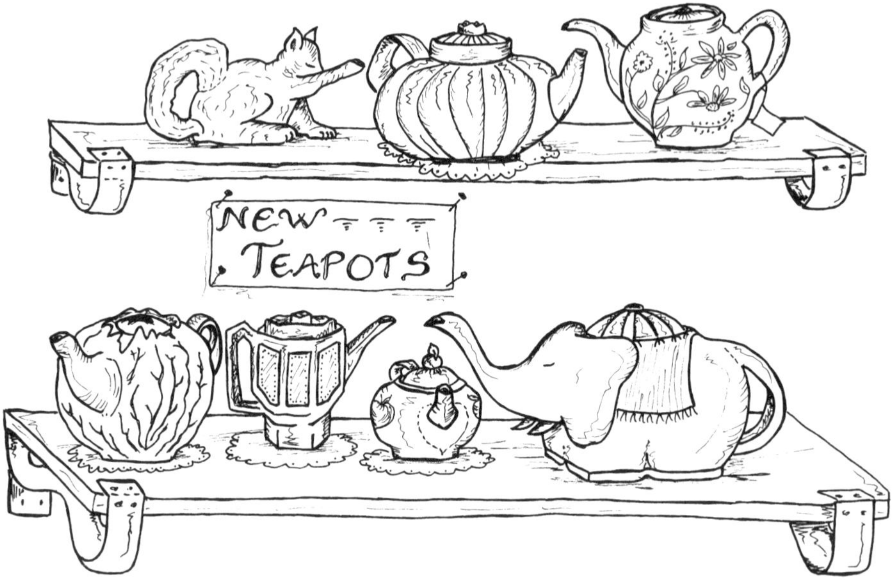
NEW
TEAPOTS

Housewife's Pride

The Chinese had porcelain for centuries
before a potter in Chelsea discovered the secret.
Soon a flood of orders for teapots
surged over Stoke-On-Trent.

Joshia Wedgwood of Staffordshire
had a good business head,
kept his prices low. Soon all
but the poorest English housewives
had his pieces gracing their tables,
invited friends for tea to show off
animal teapots or--the latest rage--
cauliflower and cabbage shapes
with Wedgewood's fine green glaze.

Dr. Samuel Johnson

                        admitted to being
"...a hardened and shameless tea drinker...
who with tea amused the evening,
with tea solaced the midnight,
and with tea welcomed the morning."

Spending evenings with friends at the Literary club
he found even his lexicographic masterpiece,
the great *Dictionary of the English Language*,
could not provide words enough to extol
all the virtues of the precious golden beverage.

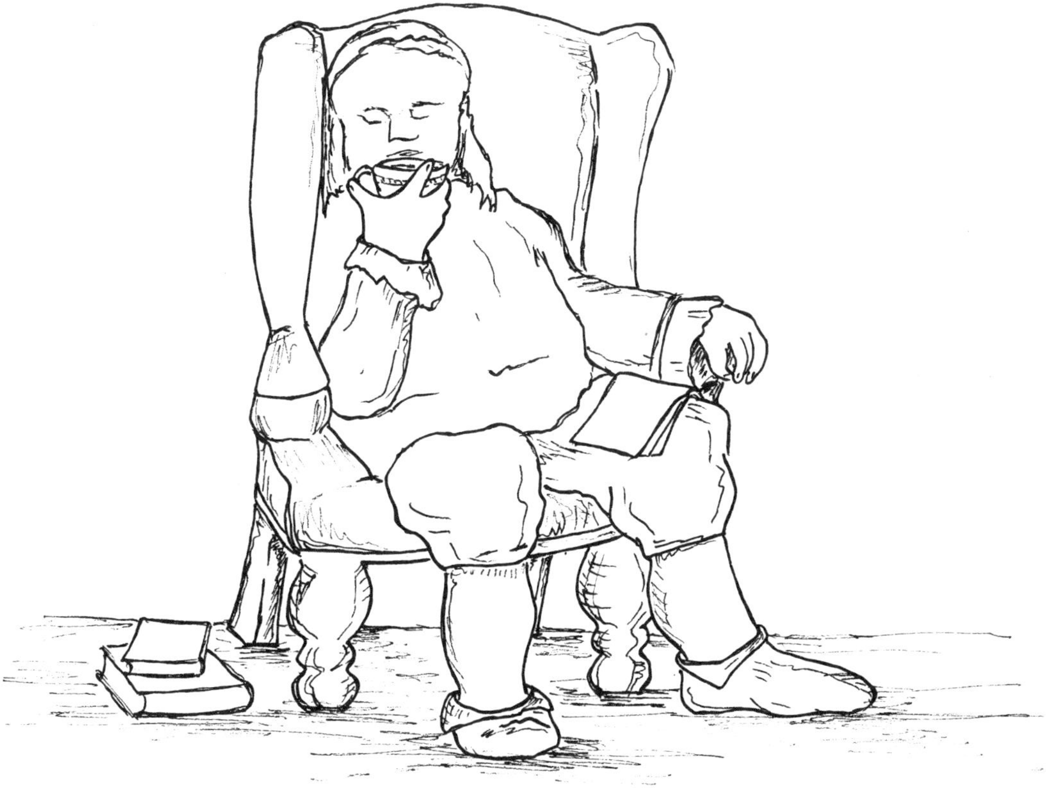

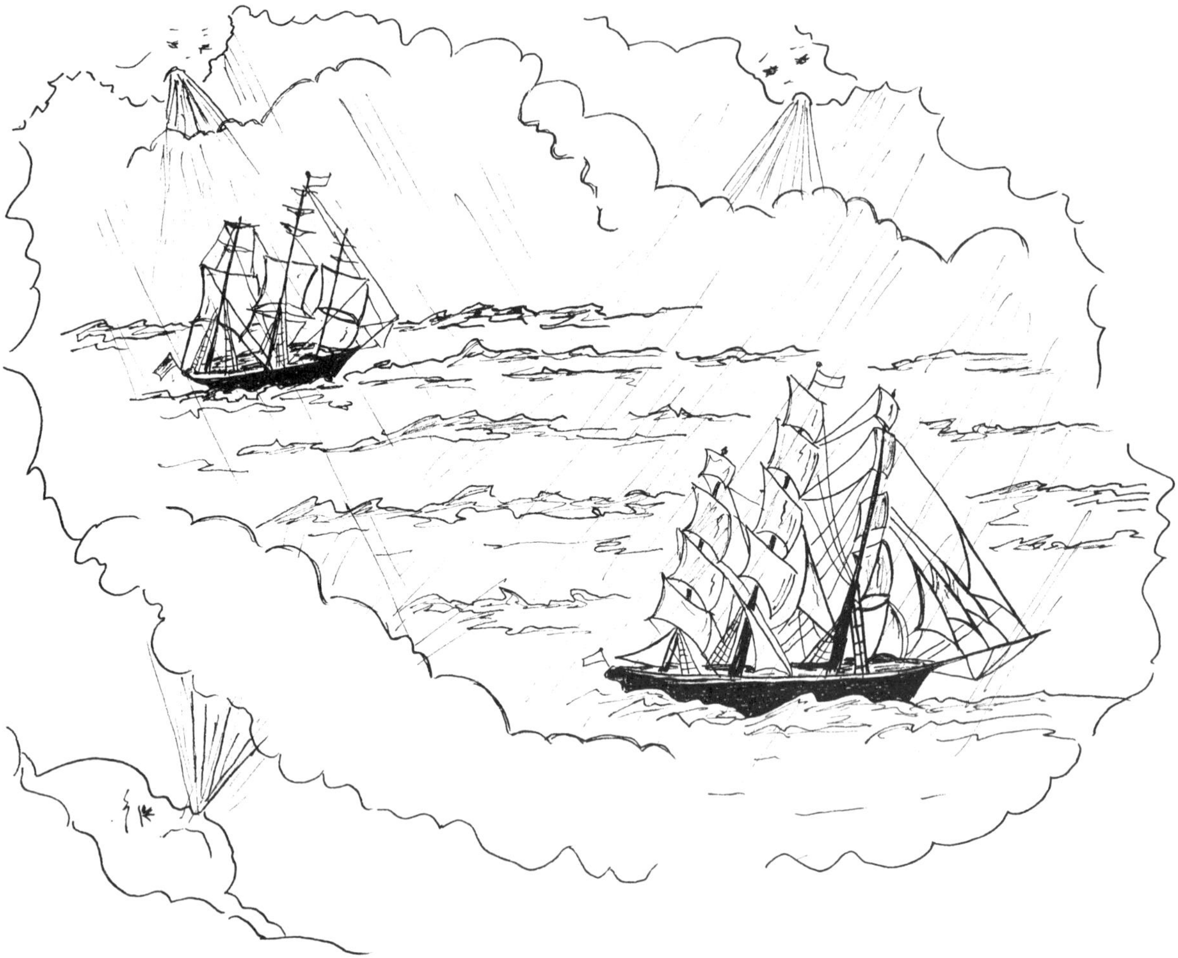

Clipper Ships

Dream of every clipper captain:
to be first up the Thames with the new season's tea!
Feverish bets, gambling riches
weighing heavily on their heads,
they push their crews to Olympian deeds.

Sails taut, running before the wind,
the Thermopylae and the Cutty Sark
race to London, the Sark 400 miles in the lead.
In the Indian Ocean a gale wind
seizes her rudder in its teeth,
dashes hopes for some wagering gentlemen
anchored safely in the chairs of their London clubs.

ICED TEA

St. Louis, Missouri, 1904

                                           104 degrees
at the Louisiana State Purchase Exposition!
No one is visiting the Far East Tea House!
Who wants a hot drink on a day like this?
Despondent promoter Richard Blechynden
is struck with an inspiration
--he pours hot tea over ice!
A newfangled idea! Word spreads quickly;
iced tea becomes the drink of the day,
perhaps the century!

Nursery Tea

Florinda and friend are taking their tea
on china that's flowered and petite.
Nursie brings jam to put on their bread
and frosted tea cakes. What a treat!

They sit up straight and try not to spill,
remembering their *thank yous* and *pleases*,
and use their napkins to wipe off the crumbs
and cover their mouths when they sneezes!

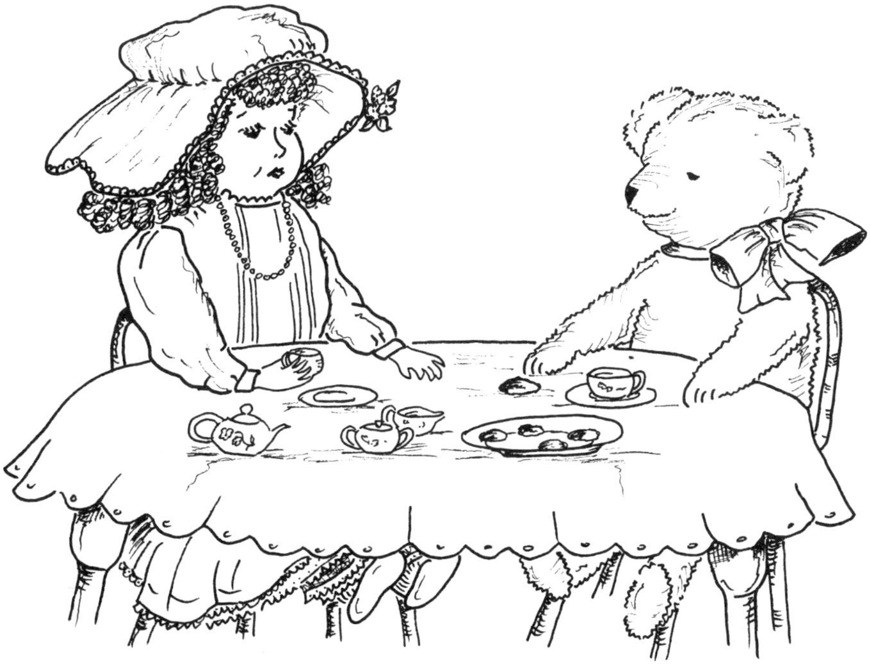

Tea Leaves Tell All

                    I see a new moon...a journey over water.

A romantic cruise! How marvie!

                    A man...a stranger...tall, dark, handsome...

Like Valentino, maybe!

                    ...standing near a wall...There is an obstacle...

Oh, golly!

                    ...but I see a ladder...It means opportunity.

Maybe I should speak first when I meet him on the cruise.

                    I see wings with an important message...
                      but clouds nearby spell disappointment.

Oh, darn...
    maybe Wally can't take me to the show at the Bijou tonight!

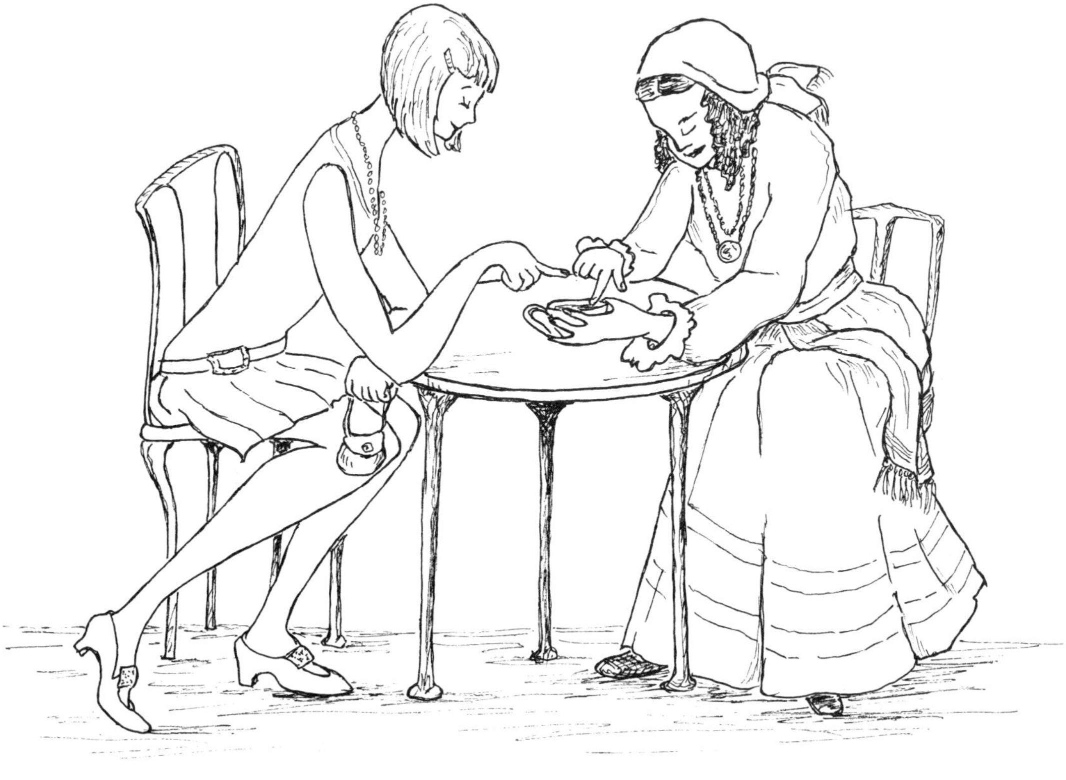

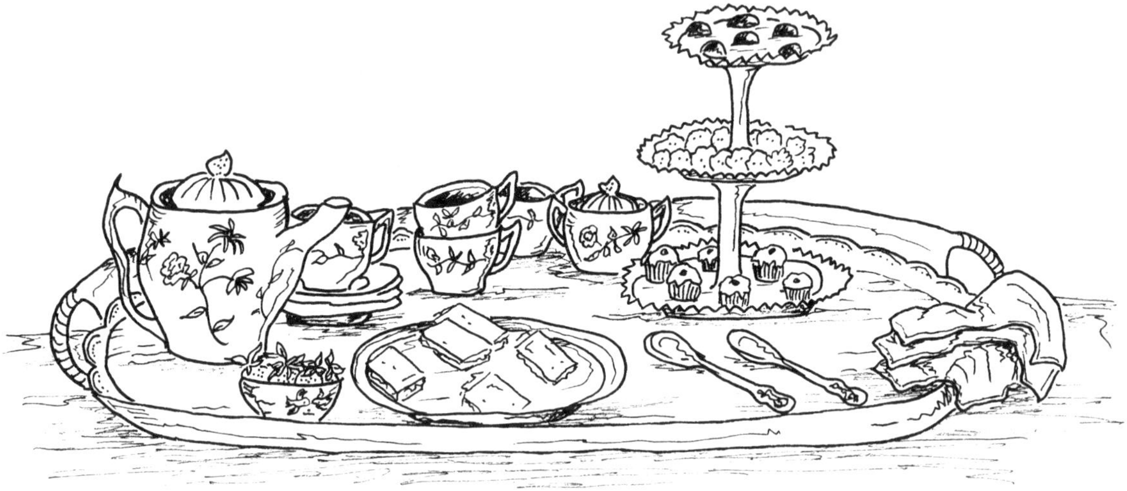

Afternoon Tea At the Ritz

Cool, proper, impeccable,
a thin green line traveling the edges
of each transparent piece
as it rests crisply
between paper thin buttered bread slices,
the cucumber sandwich
waits on a silver server
for well-groomed fingers
to pick it up, nibble daintily
with prettily spaced white teeth,
between politely measured sips
of Darjeeling and socially acceptable
conversation.

Tea Dances

> Short social events, held at a hotel
> or country club in late afternoon;
> popular in the first half of the century.

Sometimes a first date,
with parents dropping off the young pair:
he with Brilliantined hair, she with first low heels.
A piano and violin playing *Falling In Love With Love*,
Tea For Two, other sweetly romantic tunes
while he worries about sweaty hands, and she
fervently hopes her stocking seams are straight.
In painful silence broken by a gush of words
--never the sophisticated banter practiced
in the mirror at home--they dance on.
Will this piece never end? And then
it does and he follows her to the table
where tea cakes and sandwiches wait
and hands are given something useful to hold,
mouths are occupied with something
beyond conversation and relief
descends like a gentle rain from heaven.

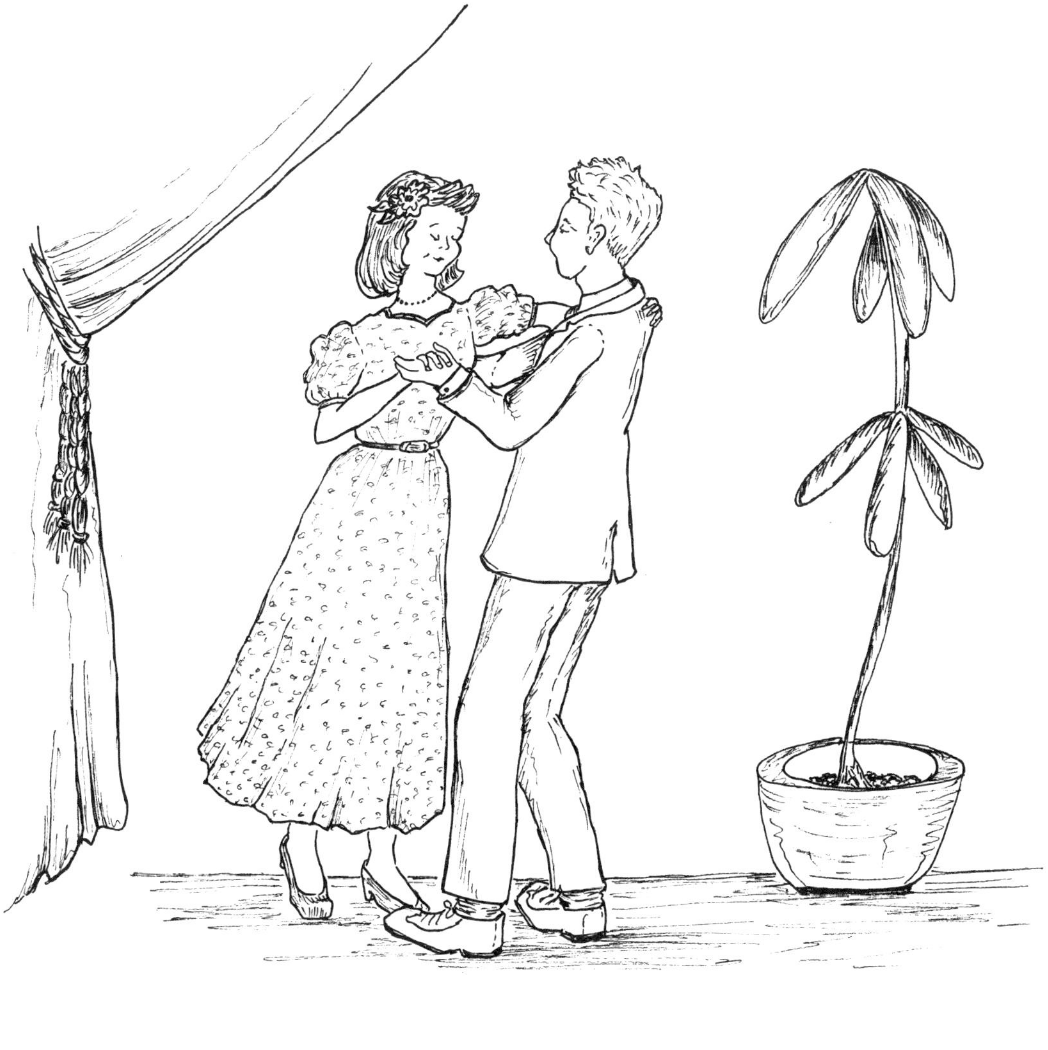

Tea Merchants

It took a year for Russian caravans loaded with furs
to travel 3000 miles to meet Chinese tea caravans
at Kyakhta, 1000 miles across the Gobi from Peking.
Exchanging loads, they retraced their long journeys
--600 pounds of tea per camel, 600 trips per year;
a hard business but lucrative at fifteen rubles per pound.

Today's tea brokers and merchants bid and purchase
in an electronic market place without traveling a single mile.
Gun Powder, Lung Ching, Keemun, Lapsang Souchong,
all appear on their screens, tested and graded;
freighters and diesel trucks furnish prompt delivery.

Exotic caravans swaying slowly across desert lands
and clipper ships running before the wind
have passed into history but the romance of Ch'a
lives on in names which flicker across screens
and labels affixed to glass jars on tea merchants' shelves:
*Dragon's Beard, Silver Needle, Handful of Snow, Pingsuey,
Spiderleg Green and Pearl Dew*--treasurable leaves
find the route to your teapot, into your cup,
a pleasurable liquid to sip and savor.

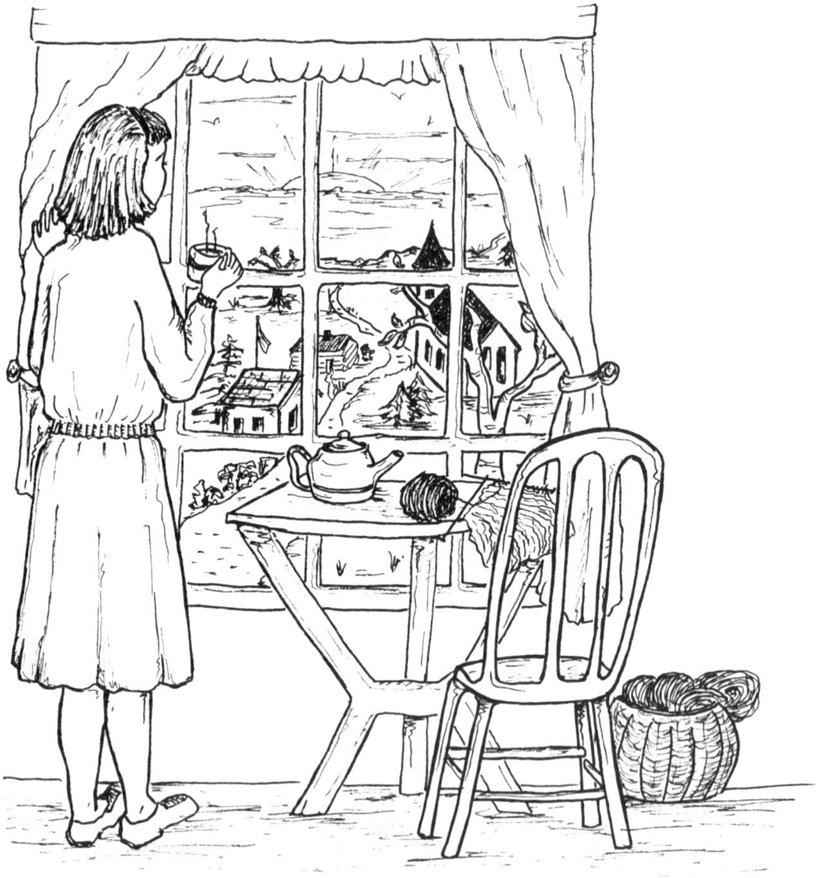

Proper Moments For Drinking Tea

when the earth is white and wind sculpts the roof
when a friend drops by
in a gazebo on a summer day
in the evening while watching old movies
when a neighbor brings warm cinnamon rolls
when you are all alone
on hot muggy afternoons
following a fine meal with guests
returning from a walk through autumn leaves
after the garden is weeded
while searching for an idea
in the morning before anyone else is up
while knitting mittens
while watching the sun set over the bay
while writing a poem

Tea Cozy

GLOSSARY

Brilliantine--Colored and perfumed dressing for making hair glossy.

Camellia sinensis (Latin)--An evergreen bush with dark green leathery leaves and fragrant white flowers. Native to hot, humid regions in Asia. Formerly named *thea sinensis,* which meant "tea of China," by early plant taxonomists.

Ch'a--The distinctive Chinese ideograph for tea appeared circa 725.

Cha-shitsu--Small Japanese garden pavilion or room within a house where the tea ceremony is observed.

Clipper ships--Fastest trading ships in the world in the mid-1800's. From them came the phrase, "moving at a good clip."

Hotel Ritz--Renowned London hotel famous for its afternoon tea since it opened in 1906 and the first to allow unescorted ladies at teatime.

Iron Goddess of Mercy--translation of Ti Kuan Yin, name of a tea in China.

Pu-erh cha--A traditional favorite Chinese tea, it has a rare exotic taste and is widely acclaimed for health benefits.

Sen-no Rikyu--A tea master who developed the first structure devoted entirely to serving and drinking tea in Japan in 1584.

Shen Nung--One of China's first emperors (a contemporary of Moses) who, according to popular legend, is credited with discovering tea as a beverage.

Tea Cozy (Scot. cosie)--A padded covering for a teapot to help it retain heat. They are often made by mothers and grandmothers to put into a bride's hope chest.

Tribute tea--Presented to the Chinese emperor during the 8th century. As it's popularity spread, tribute tea was fired, powdered, pressed into a paste and, finally, molded into cakes in order to transport it in large quantities.

References used in research:

Campbell, Dawn L., *The Tea Book*.
  Gretna, LA: Pelican Pub., 1995.

Knight, Elizabeth, *Tea With Friends*.
  Pownal, VT: Storey Books, 1998.

Pratt, James N., *The Tea Lover's Treasury*.
  San Ramon, CT: 101 Productions, 1982.

Whipple, A.B.C., *The Clipper Ships*.
  Time Life Books, Alexandra, VA: 1980.

Johnson Editions, Ltd., *A Proper Tea*.
  St. Martin's Press, NY: 1987.

Periodical: *Tea Talk*.
  Madison, WI: The Tea Man, 1998.

Acknowledgments:

We are grateful for the help of the following people:

Nancy Davis--photography.

The Poets' Group--for their help in critiquing, especially Sue DeKelver who checked all of the poems "one last time."

George--who helped on the computer and chauffeured.

Ellen Kort--for her support.

Chas Maring--who guided us through the world of book publishing.